HAL LEONARD

BASS METHOD BOOK 2

SECOND EDITION

BY ED FRIEDLAND

The Box Shape 2
   E, A & B Box 3
   Box Lunch..................................... 3
   Box-E Blues 3
Movable Boxes 4
   Your Move 5
   Move It.. 5
   Movie Star 5
5th Position...................................... 6
On the G String 6
Shift Practice.................................... 7
   Shifty Henry 7
On the D String 8
   Dee Gee 8
   5-3-1.. 9
   Dig It 9
Introducing Tablature............................ 10
On the A String 10
   Tab Hunter 11
   Pay the Tab 11
On the E String 12
   Open/Closed................................... 13
   Da Blues...................................... 13
   All Together Now 14
   Swing Time 15
One Finger Per Fret 15
The Major Scale 16
   Scale Sequence #1 17
   Scale Sequence #2 17
Key Signatures 18
Universal Fingerings 20
   Scale Sequence #3 21
   Scale Sequence #4 21
   Pasta Mon 22
   D-Lish 22
   A-Flat Tire 22
   Open E 23
   G3 23
   B-Flat Jump 23
The Classic Blues Line........................... 24
   Gee Blues..................................... 24
   Aay, Blues!................................... 24
   Low Down 25

Understanding Bass Lines 25
Syncopated Eighth Notes 26
   Off Beat 27
   Funky Soul Groove 27
   That '70s Thing.............................. 27
The Major Triad................................... 28
   Tri Again 31
   Funky Li'l Blues.............................. 31
The Minor Scale 32
   Minor Scale Sequence......................... 32
   Relative Major and Minor 32
   House O' Horror............................... 35
   Noir 35
   Jazz Minor 35
Modulation 36
   Minor Modulation 36
   Mod Crazy..................................... 36
Minor Triads 37
   Bogey Man 40
   Roots 40
   Gypsy Swing................................... 41
   Room-ba with a View.......................... 41
Eighth-Note Triplets............................. 42
   The '50s...................................... 43
12/8 Time 43
   Bumpin' 43
The Shuffle Rhythm 44
   Old Days...................................... 44
One- and Two-Measure Repeats 45
   Bad Bone 45
   Uptown Down................................... 45
   Classic Flat 7 46
   Rollin'....................................... 46
   Go On... 47

PLAYBACK+

Speed • Pitch • Balance • Loop

To access audio visit:
www.halleonard.com/mylibrary

Enter Code
1876-1904-0429-0157

ISBN 978-0-7935-6379-1

 Each track is recorded in stereo, with bass panned hard right. To remove the bass, adjust the balance control on your playback device or computer.

All instruments performed by Ed Friedland.
Edited by Doug Downing

HAL•LEONARD®
CORPORATION
7777 W. BLUEMOUND RD. P.O. BOX 13819 MILWAUKEE, WI 53213

THE BOX SHAPE

The **box shape** is a common four-note pattern found in all styles of bass playing. It forms a square shape on the fingerboard that can be easily moved. The lowest note in the pattern is the root, and the highest note is the octave.

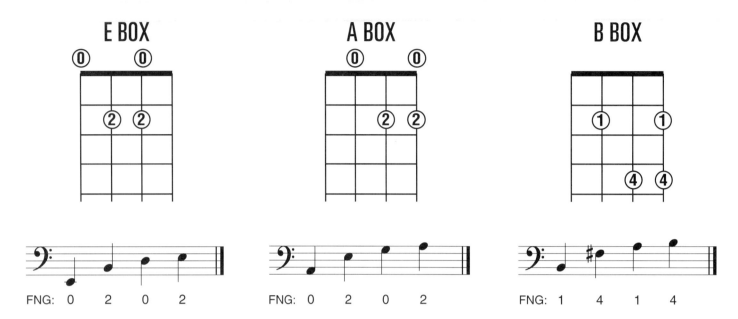

For octave jumps off the E string, place the right-hand thumb on the E string while playing the higher notes on the D string. Use the left hand to mute the open D string in measure 3.

For octave jumps off the A string, rest the right thumb on the A string and lean it against the E string while playing the higher notes on the G string. Use the left hand to mute the open G string in measure 3.

The B box has no open strings—so the fingering can be moved around the fingerboard easily. More on that soon.

TRACK 1

TUNING NOTES

E, A & B BOX

TRACK 2
SLOW/FAST

BOX LUNCH

TRACK 3

BOX-E BLUES

TRACK 4

MOVABLE BOXES

Movable boxes all have the same fingering. Place your 1st finger on any note on the E or A string; that becomes the root. The box shape for that root follows the fingering pattern shown below. Movable box patterns can be used to create your own bass lines.

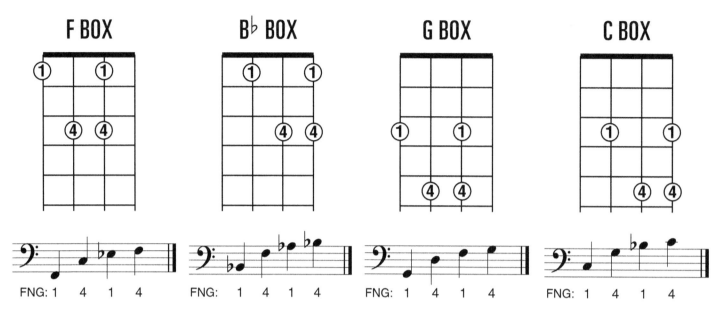

Remember to keep your left hand relaxed as you play. If these shapes feel like a stretch, let your hand pivot naturally at the thumb when moving between lower and higher notes.

The following examples show a one-measure box pattern. When you've learned the pattern thoroughly, play through the example by moving the pattern to the correct root, as indicated by the chord symbol above each measure.

YOUR MOVE

TRACK 5

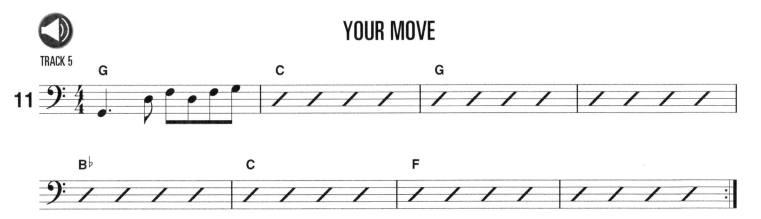

To play the F♯ box shape in this example, move your hand down to the 2nd fret.

MOVE IT

TRACK 6
SLOW/FAST

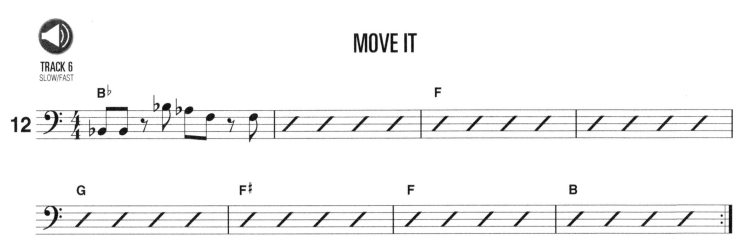

While the pattern remains the same, the A and E chords use the open E and A strings for their roots. Pay attention to muting your open strings.

MOVIE STAR

TRACK 7

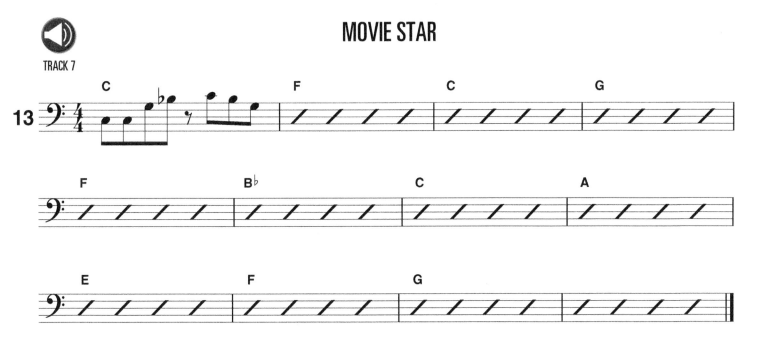

5TH POSITION

So far, we've played in 1st, 2nd, and 3rd positions. Let's continue to expand our knowledge of the fingerboard; playing in 5th position will give us access to a few new notes as well as alternate fingerings for notes we've already learned.

ON THE G STRING

Place your first finger on the 5th fret of the G string. We are still using the 1-2-4 fingering system.

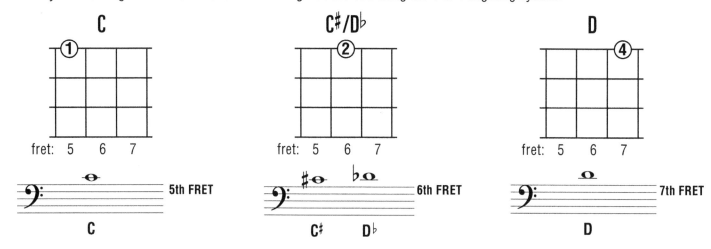

To get more comfortable with the notes in this position, say them aloud as you play: "C, C♯, D..."

This example uses the open G string—keep the hand in 5th position and play the open string.

SHIFT PRACTICE

Many bass lines require you to play in several positions. It's important to be comfortable shifting between positions. Release the finger pressure before making the shift, and land on the new note as gently as possible.

Practice the shifts in example A individually, back and forth. Make the shifts as smooth as possible. Example B shifts from 5th position down to the open G, and back up.

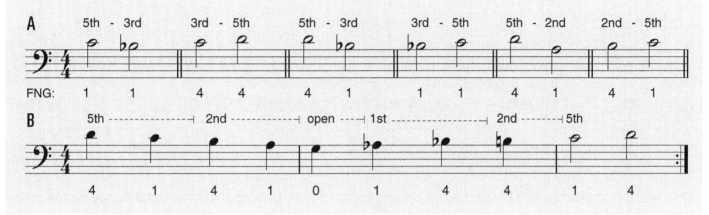

This example shifts between 3rd and 5th position.

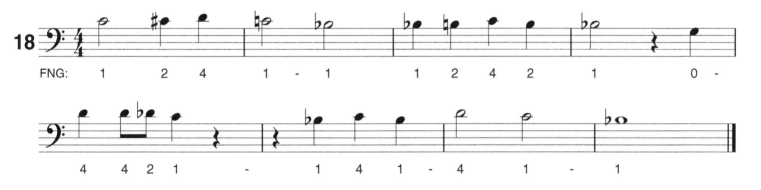

This example has many shifts. The important fingerings are marked, and all shifts are indicated by the "-" symbol.

TRACK 8

SHIFTY HENRY

ON THE D STRING

Here are the notes in 5th position on the D string.

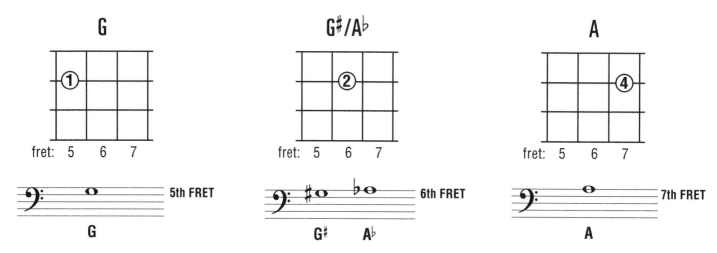

You'll recall these notes can also be found on the G string (open, 1st fret, and 2nd fret). Which position you choose to play them in will depend on the notes occurring before and after. For now, they'll be read in 5th position.

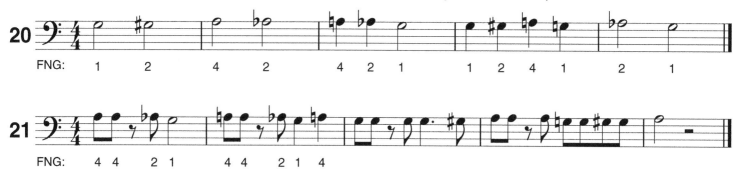

This example uses the open D string; stay in 5th position.

This example starts on open D, but it is still played in 5th position.

TRACK 9

DEE GEE

8

Now practice playing across the D and G strings in 5th position.

This one crosses the D and G strings and "bounces" down to open D. Remember, it's all in 5th position.

Play on the D and G strings and shift between 5th, 3rd, and 1st positions. Remember: 3/4 time means 3 beats per bar.

TRACK 10

5-3-1

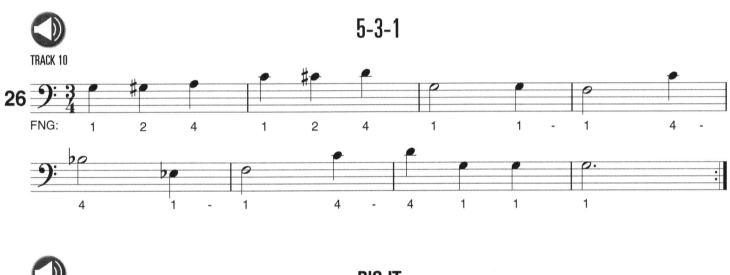

TRACK 11

DIG IT

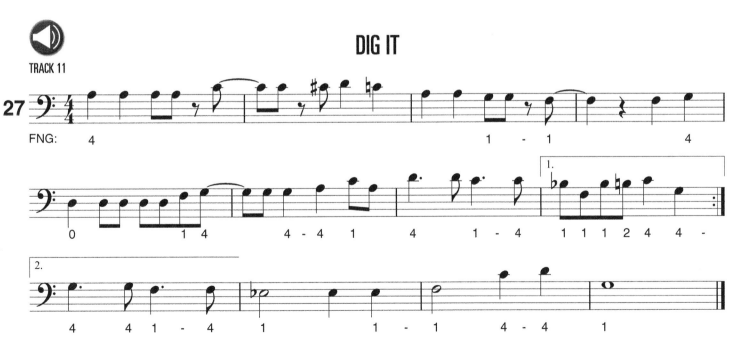

ON THE A STRING

Here are the notes on the A string in 5th position. These notes are also available on the D string: open, 1st fret, and 2nd fret. For now, we'll stick to 5th position locations.

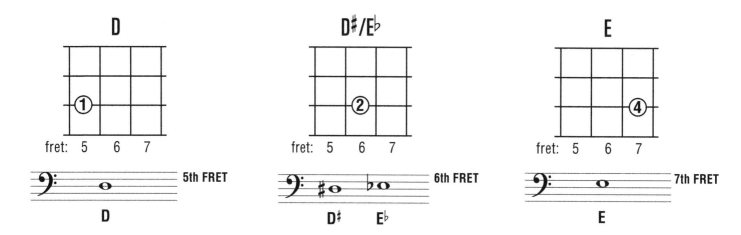

This example bounces off the open A string but stays in 5th position.

INTRODUCING TABLATURE

Tablature is a system of notating the specific location of notes on the fingerboard. In 5th position, there are many notes that could be played elsewhere on the neck; tablature (or "tab") is a handy way to indicate where they are best played.

The tab staff is 4 lines: the bottom line represents the E string; the next line is the A string, then the D string, and then the G string. Numbers on the lines represent frets. For each note on the staff, there will be a number in tab indicating the exact fret location of that note.

This example uses tablature to clearly indicate where the notes are played.

TAB HUNTER

TRACK 12

This crosses the A, D, and G strings, and shifts between 5th and 3rd positions. Tablature makes it clear.

PAY THE TAB

TRACK 13

ON THE E STRING

Here are the notes on the E string in 5th position. These notes are also found on the A string: open, 1st fret, and 2nd fret. These examples use 5th position.

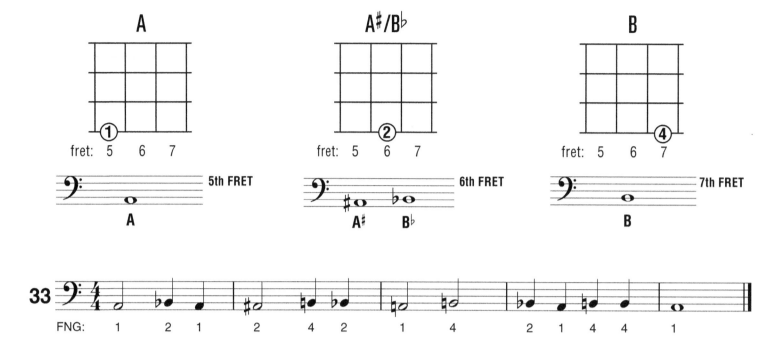

This stays in 5th position, but bounces down to the open E string.

Now play all the notes in 5th position across all 4 strings.

Crossing all four strings in 5th position, this one has some unusual switches between the open strings and their fretted counterparts. Check the tab carefully.

Here is a tune that shifts between several positions and crosses all four strings. Follow the tab, and experiment with different fingerings. Once you've got the fingerings down for this piece, practice reading it without looking at the tab. You'll develop a better sense of what you're playing and you'll keep up your note-reading "chops."

ALL TOGETHER NOW

This is an example of a **walking bass line**. The constant quarter-note rhythm and non-repetitive note choices give it a distinct jazz flavor. This piece starts in 1st position, shifts up to 5th, and then shifts back down to 1st. Open strings are used to make the shifts easier. Try reading it first without looking at the tab, and see how well you do.

SWING TIME

ONE FINGER PER FRET

Another fingering system commonly used on the bass assigns one finger to each fret. This expands what is available under your hand by one more note. This system is *not* advisable for box shapes as it puts too much strain on the hand. To use OFPF without strain, you must learn to use the **pivot** in the left hand between the 2nd and 3rd finger. Play a note with the 1st finger, then lay down the 2nd finger. When moving to the 3rd finger, release the 1st finger and pivot slightly on the 2nd finger and thumb to reach the note with the 3rd finger. Lay down the 4th finger next. Pivoting like this eliminates the need to stretch the hand open to reach the notes. Extended periods of stretching open your hand can be painful and potentially damaging. Stay relaxed and flexible as much as possible.

Practice playing across all four strings with OFPF. When you've reached the last note, reverse directions and come back down.

THE MAJOR SCALE

The **major scale** is a group of 8 notes that occur in a specific order. It is the basis of most popular music and is an important tool in developing an understanding of how music is structured.

The major scale is constructed by combining *whole steps* (the distance between 2 frets) and *half steps* (1 fret) in this pattern:

C MAJOR SCALE

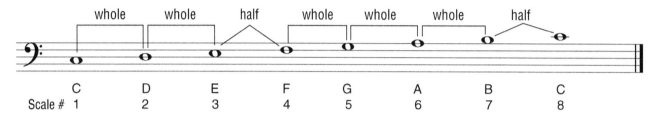

Each note in the scale is numbered 1 through 8. The 1st (and 8th) note is called the root or tonic (in this case, C). It is the note that gives the scale its name or **key**, and sounds like "home base." The numerical system is used to describe melodies, root motion, and many other musical elements.

Using the OFPF system and starting on the 2nd finger, the major scale falls naturally under the hand in one position. This is the "**universal fingering**" for the major scale; it will produce the scale in any key starting from the 2nd fret and above on the E or A strings. Here it is in C major.

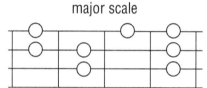
major scale

Remember: When using the OFPF system to play notes in a single position like this, allow your left hand to pivot naturally between the 2nd and 3rd fingers; always keep the hand relaxed.

The next two examples use the number system exclusively. Using the universal fingering in the key of C position, play the notes that correspond to the scale numbers. Say the scale numbers aloud. Pay attention to the note names as well.

TRACK 18

SCALE SEQUENCE #1

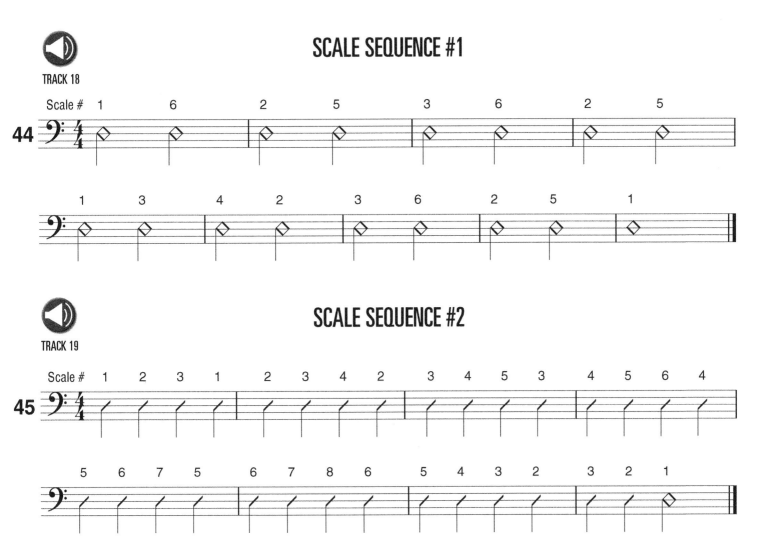

TRACK 19

SCALE SEQUENCE #2

If you examine the notes in the key of C, you'll notice that there are no sharps or flats. The half steps in the scale (between 3 & 4 and 7 & 8) naturally occur between E & F and B & C. In different keys, it is necessary to add sharps or flats to maintain the sequence of whole and half steps that produce the major scale.

Each new key has its own unique **key signature** that indicates which notes are sharp or flat. It appears at the beginning of a line of music. Here are the key signatures for keys up to 5 sharps and 5 flats.

Sharps or flats indicated in the key signature are played automatically unless cancelled out by a natural sign (♮).

To get familiar with the above keys, play them first in **open position**—that is, starting on the lowest possible root on the fingerboard, and using as many open strings as possible. Some of these keys/scales will be easier to play this way than others. The keys of G, A, E, F, and B♭ will be especially useful. Use the 1-2-4 fingering system, and refer to the fingerings and shifts as needed.

Play each scale several times, and be sure to watch for sharps and flats. Say the note names as you play.

In 2nd position.

G MAJOR

Start in 2nd position; shift up to 5th position.

D MAJOR

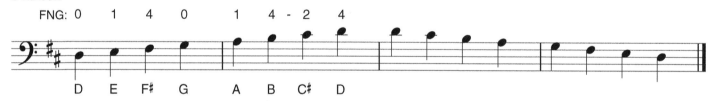

Start in 2nd position; shift down to 1st position.

A MAJOR

Start in 2nd position; shift down to 1st position.

E MAJOR

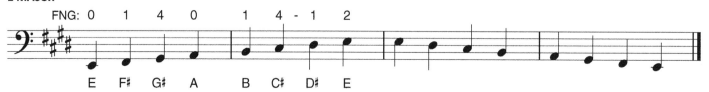

Try the OPFP system for this one. (Start on the 2nd fret, A string.)

B MAJOR

FNG: 2 4 1 2 4 1 3 4

B C# D# E F# G# A# B

In 1st position.

F MAJOR

FNG: 1 4 0 1 4 0 2 4

F G A B♭ C D E F

In 1st position.

B♭ MAJOR

FNG: 1 4 0 1 4 0 2 4

B♭ C D E♭ F G A B♭

Start in 1st position; shift up to 5th (with a stretch).

E♭ MAJOR

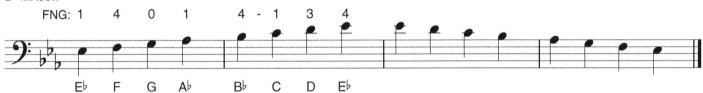

FNG: 1 4 0 1 4 - 1 3 4

E♭ F G A♭ B♭ C D E♭

In 1st position. (Use OFPF at the start.)

A♭ MAJOR

FNG: 4 1 3 4 - 1 4 0 1

A♭ B♭ C D♭ E♭ F G A♭

Start in 1st position, then shift up. (Again, try OFPF at the start.)

D♭ MAJOR

FNG: 4 1 3 4 1 4 - 2 4

D♭ E♭ F G♭ A♭ B♭ C D♭

TIP: Before playing any piece of music, check the key signature. Play the corresponding scale up and down, saying the note names aloud. You'll be warmed up and ready to play!

UNIVERSAL FINGERINGS

Of course, all the major keys can also be played with the universal fingering (2-4, 1-2-4, 1-3-4). E, B, F, and E♭ are in higher positions than you've learned, but it's simple to plug in the fingering and play the scale.

Again, play each scale several times. First say the note names, then the scale numbers.

Start on the 3rd fret, E string.

G MAJOR

Start on the 5th fret, A string.

D MAJOR

Start on the 5th fret, E string.

A MAJOR

Start on the 7th fret, A string.

E MAJOR

Start on the 7th fret, E string.

B MAJOR

Start on the 8th fret, A string.

F MAJOR

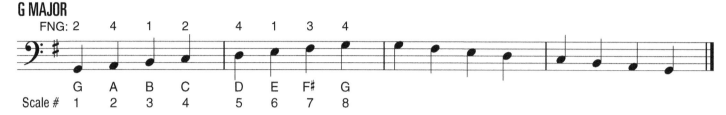

Start on the 6th fret fret, E string.

B♭ MAJOR

B♭   C   D   E♭   F   G   A   B♭

Start on the 6th fret, A string.

E♭ MAJOR

E♭   F   G   A♭   B♭   C   D   E♭

Start on the 4th fret, E string.

A♭ MAJOR

A♭   B♭   C   D♭   E♭   F   G   A♭

Start on the 4th fret, A string.

D♭ MAJOR

D♭   E♭   F   G♭   A♭   B♭   C   D♭

Once you are comfortable with each scale in its various positions, play them all using these numerical sequences. For more practice in this area, go back to Scale Sequences #1 and #2 and play them in all keys.

SCALE SEQUENCE #3

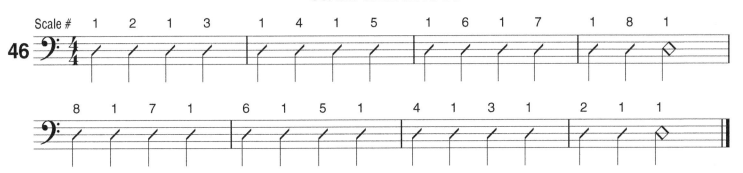

SCALE SEQUENCE #4

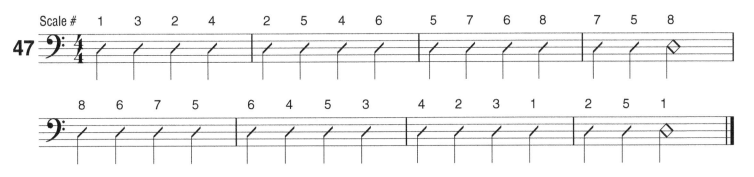

Now it's time to play. Check the key signature, and play the sharps and flats as indicated. Find your own fingerings.

TRACK 20

PASTA MON

While the notes in this next piece go below the root D, it is still playable in the D major scale position at the 5th fret. You could consider this a "lower extension" of the universal fingering. The piece can also be played in open position.

major scale
(w/lower extension)

TRACK 21
SLOW/FAST

D-LISH

Try this in the universal scale fingering; you can also read it in open position.

TRACK 22

A-FLAT TIRE

OPEN E

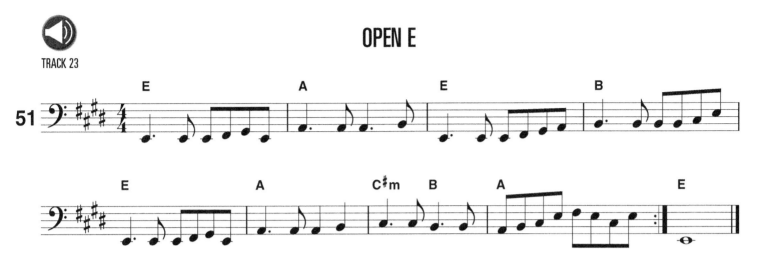

This can be played in open G and universal positions. Try them both.

G3

This, too, can be played in open and universal positions.

B-FLAT JUMP

THE CLASSIC BLUES LINE

This very familiar bass line follows a pattern that fits right into the universal scale fingering, making it very easy to play in any key. Hint: You'll need an upper extension for the C7 and D7 chords. (Refer to the diagram below.)

In this key, the line can also be played in open position; try it both ways.

TRACK 26

GEE BLUES

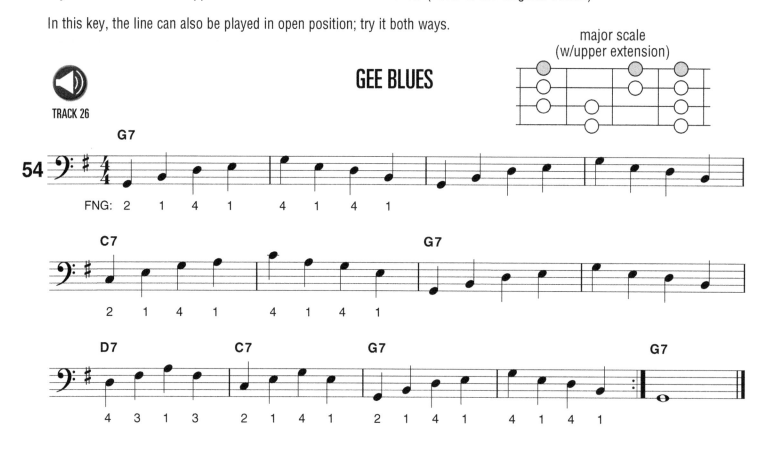

This line has variations in the main pattern and in measures 9 through 12. They are interchangeable with the original line. The key of A can also be played in open position, but measures 9 and 10 need to be repositioned. Can you figure out how to do it?

TRACK 27

AAY, BLUES!

E is a very popular key for the blues. Shifting the classic line into E requires you to play in open position. This version is a "doubled up" rhythm using eighth notes. This has a more "rock 'n' roll" feel to it, but the line is the same as the original.

LOW DOWN

TRACK 28

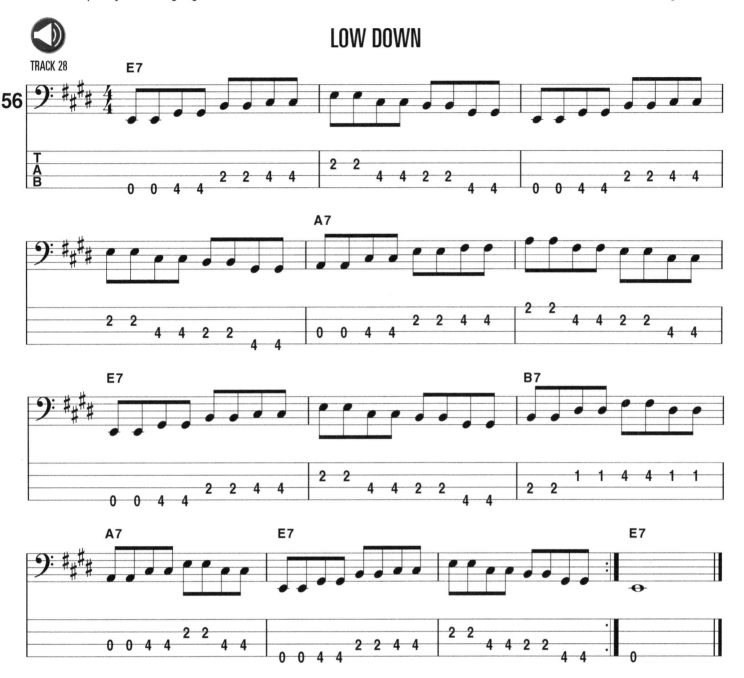

UNDERSTANDING BASS LINES

An effective way to understand bass lines is to determine the scale numbers that represent the notes. By now you can figure out the scale numbers within a key, but when chords change, you'll sometimes find it easier to think of the notes in relationship to the new chord. The root of each new chord becomes scale number 1. In the example below, the scale numbers on the E7 chord are 1-3-5-6-8-5-3. When it moves to the A7 chord, the A (the root) becomes the new number 1, so the pattern for the A7 chord is also 1-3-5-6-8-6-5-3.

Rather than figure out the numbers for the entire line in the key of E, each new chord represents a separate "key"—not literally, but in terms of playing and understanding the line. This approach can be especially effective in playing blues.

SYNCOPATED EIGHTH NOTES

Syncopation is the placement of rhythmic accents on weak beats or weak portions of beats. Syncopated eighth notes, for example, emphasize the upbeat, or "and" of a beat. They are an important part of rock, blues, funk, R&B, soul, latin, jazz, and even country music.

Practice these slowly, counting the eighth notes aloud "1 + 2 +" etc. In order for syncopation to sound correct, the downbeats need to be felt. Once you are comfortable with the rhythms, use a metronome clicking on quarter notes.

Fingerstyle players, remember to alternate between index (i) and middle (m) fingers. To mute the string during a rest, place the alterate finger down early—stopping the string's vibration—before playing the next note. Pick style players, continue to use downstrokes on downbeats, and upstrokes on upbeats (or play all downstrokes, if you prefer). Be sure to mute all rests with your left hand.

OFF BEAT

FUNKY SOUL GROOVE

THAT '70S THING

THE MAJOR TRIAD

A *major triad* is a three-note chord structure built with the root, 3rd, and 5th notes of the major scale.

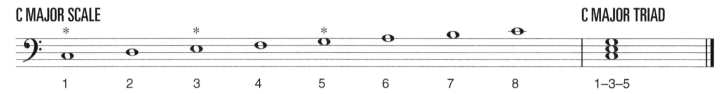

On instruments like guitar and piano, chords are typically played with all notes ringing at the same time. On bass, they are played in a melodic sequence, called an *arpeggio*. Arpeggios are used in bass lines to outline the chords of a song.

Major triads can be played in all keys within the universal scale position. The octave is added but isn't considered a new note as it is the same as the root.

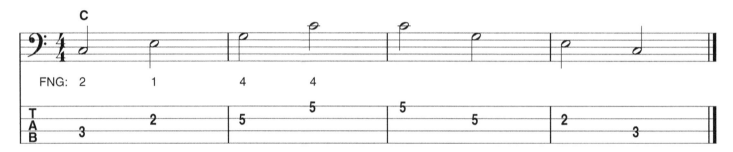

But they can also be played this way in any key: Don't try to stretch for the 3rd of the chord; shift up to the 4th finger.

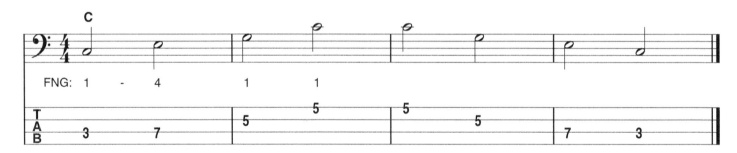

In many keys, open strings are also available.

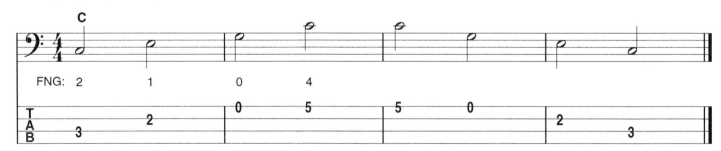

When deciding which fingering to use, consider which is most convenient to play, but also consider which sounds better.

Here are the *flat key* major triads with various fingerings. Practice them each way several times, say the note names, and the scale numbers. Once familiar, use a metronome clicking quarter notes.

Here are the *sharp key* major triads in various fingerings. Practice them the same way.

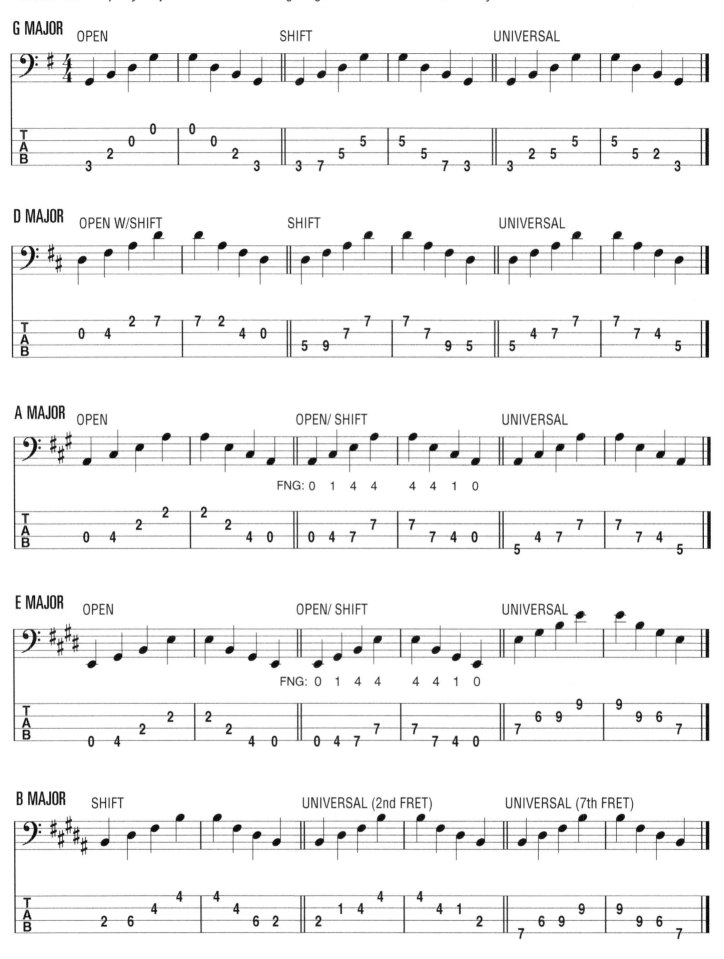

Triads are very effective for outlining a chord progression; they are a classic approach to constructing a bass line.

TRI AGAIN

TRACK 32

Remember how D.C. al Coda and Coda signs work? In the piece above, take the repeat sign back to letter A; next time, go on to letter B. When you reach the D.C. al Coda indication, go back to the top of the song and play until the To Coda (⊕) indication. From there, skip to the Coda at the end of the song.

This example takes the basic triad and adds an additional note, the **6th**, for a slightly different type of line.

FUNKY LI'L BLUES

TRACK 33

THE MINOR SCALE

The **minor scale** has a flatted 3rd scale degree, which gives it a "sadder" quality compared to major. While there are several types of minor scale, we'll learn what's called "natural minor." In addition to the flatted 3rd, it also has flatted 6th and 7th degrees.

C NATURAL MINOR

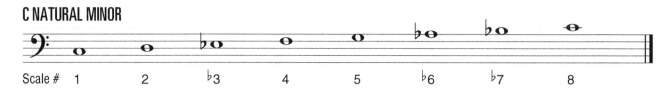

The natural minor scale also has a universal fingering that will work in any key. It uses the OFPF system and starts on the 1st finger.

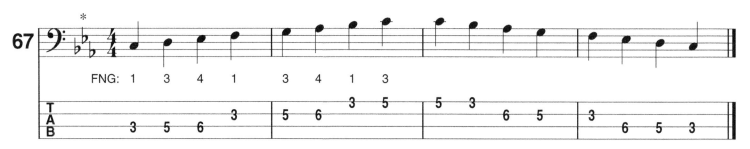

Practice the natural minor scale first saying the note names, then saying the scale numbers. Also practice it using this scale sequence.

TRACK 34

MINOR SCALE SEQUENCE

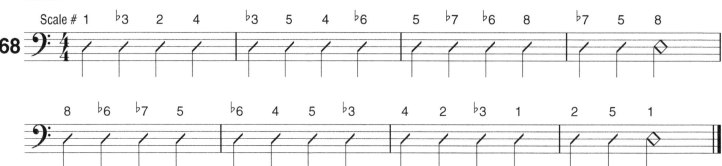

RELATIVE MINOR AND MAJOR

The natural minor scale and the major scale are related to one another. Play the C major scale; the 6th note is A. Now play A natural minor. It contains the same exact notes as C major. This is because A minor is the **relative minor** of C major. They share the same key signature.

To find the relative minor of any major key, count down to the 6th scale degree of that major scale. In reverse, to find the relative major of any minor key, count up to the flat 3rd of that minor scale.

*Understanding how the relative major/minor concept works, you now see that the proper key signature for C minor is actually the same as the key signature for E♭ major: that is, three flats.

To get familiar with the natural minor keys, let's play them first in open position—where possible—and then in the universal natural minor fingering: 1-3-4, 1-3-4, 1-3. Say the note names as you play, and then the scale numbers.

First, here is A minor. Start on the open A string for open position; on the 5th fret, E string for universal fingering.

A MINOR

A   B   C   D   E   F   G   A

Now try the *flat key* natural minor scales.

Start on open D for open position; on the 5th fret, A string for universal.

D MINOR

D   E   F   G   A   B♭   C   D

Start on 3rd fret, E string for open position or universal.

G MINOR

G   A   B♭   C   D   E♭   F   G

Start on 3rd fret, A string for open position or universal.

C MINOR

C   D   E♭   F   G   A♭   B♭   C

Start on 1st fret, E string for universal. Also try one octave higher, at the 8th fret, A string.

F MINOR

F   G   A♭   B♭   C   D♭   E♭   F

Start on 1st fret, A string or 6th fret, E string.

B♭ MINOR

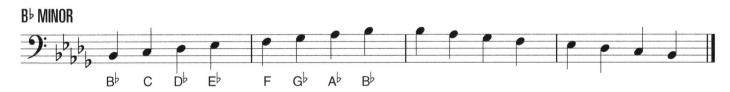

B♭   C   D♭   E♭   F   G♭   A♭   B♭

Here are the *sharp key* natural minor scales.

Start on open E for open position; at the 7th fret, A string for universal (one octave higher).

E MINOR

E   F#   G   A   B   C   D   E

Start on 2nd fret, A string for open position or universal. Start on 7th fret, E string for universal.

B MINOR

B   C#   D   E   F#   G   A   B

Start on 2nd fret, E string.

F# MINOR

F#   G#   A   B   C#   D   E   F#

Start on 4th fret, A string.

C# MINOR

C#   D#   E   F#   G#   A   B   C#

Start on 4th fret, E string.

G# MINOR

G#   A#   B   C#   D#   E   F#   G#

For more practice with the minor scales, be sure to play them using the Minor Scale Sequence (on page 32). Here are diagrams of the universal fingering for the minor scale (as well as a lower extension) for your reference:

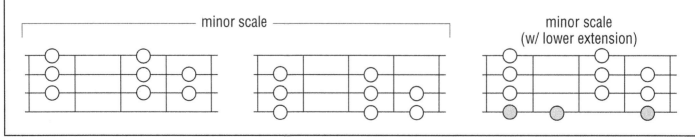

minor scale

minor scale
(w/ lower extension)

Identify the keys below. Play the corresponding minor scale, in open or in universal position, saying the note names aloud. Then play the piece.

HOUSE O' HORROR

TRACK 35
SLOW/FAST

NOIR

TRACK 36
SLOW/FAST

JAZZ MINOR

TRACK 37

MODULATION

When a piece of music changes key, it's called a **modulation**. The new key signature is displayed on the staff, and all the new accidentals for that key are in effect until another modulation occurs.

MINOR MODULATION

TRACK 38

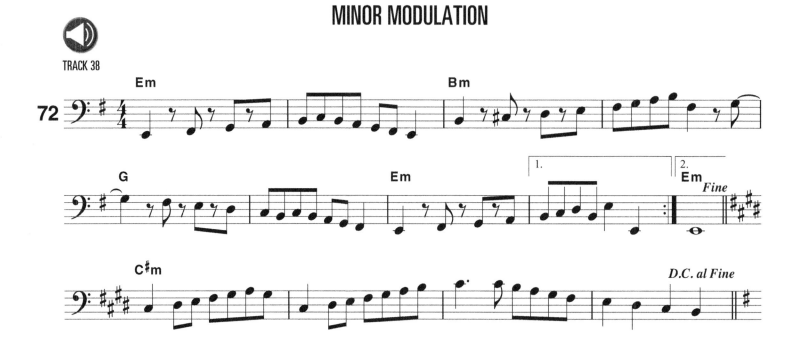

This scale exercise modulates every two measures. Keep careful track of the new accidentals as they appear.

TRACK 39

MOD CRAZY

MINOR TRIADS

Minor triads are built from the minor scale using the root, flat 3rd, and 5th notes.

Minor triads also have a universal fingering that works in all keys. Again, we add the octave on top.

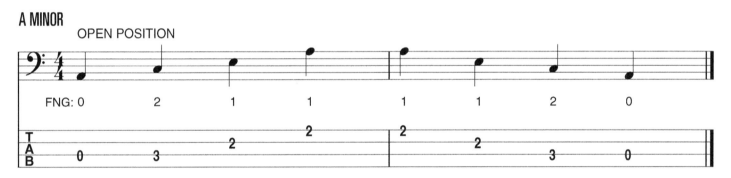

Many minor triads can also be played in open position.

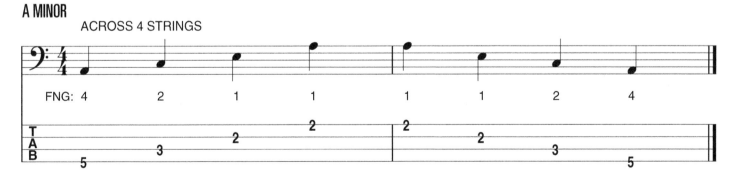

Another fingering that is a bit tricky spans across all four strings.

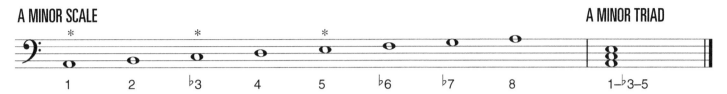

Here are the sharp key minor triads with various fingerings. Practice them each way several times, saying the note names and scale numbers. Once they are familiar, use a metronome clicking quarter notes.

Here are the flat key minor triads.

Use your knowledge of triads—both minor and major—to play through these next pieces.

TRACK 40

BOGEY MAN

This reggae tune has a tricky modulation, from 5 sharps to 4 flats.

TRACK 41

ROOTS

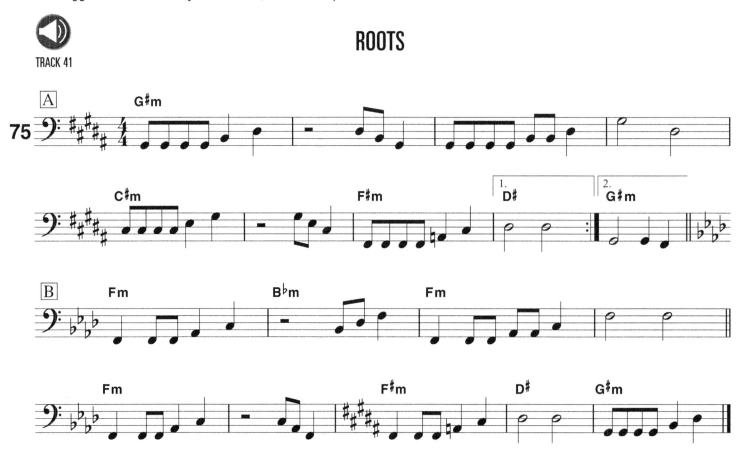

Often songs in minor keys will modulate to the relative major key. This has a swingy, old time jazz feel; give the eighth notes a bouncy feel.

GYPSY SWING

TRACK 42

Of course, minor triads are not restricted to minor keys. This rhumba in G major includes several minor triads.

ROOM-BA WITH A VIEW

TRACK 43

EIGHTH-NOTE TRIPLETS

Triplets manage to squeeze three notes into the space of one. For example, instead of dividing the quarter note in half as in regular eighth notes, it is split into thirds—resulting in eighth-note triplets.

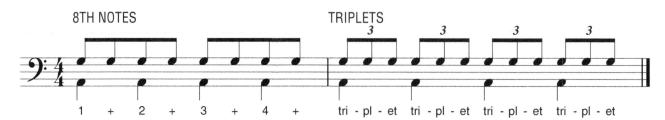

Evenly space the word "tri-pl-et" starting on each quarter note; make sure they feel relaxed and "round." In pick style playing, triplets can represent a real challenge. Be sure to keep downstrokes on downbeats (1, 2, 3, and 4). This means either playing all downstrokes, or using a downstroke-upstroke-downstroke combination.

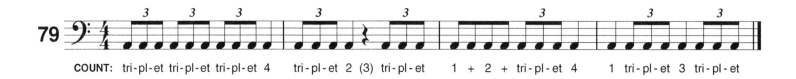

Triplets can also be written with a connecting bracket—for example, if there is a rest within the triplet. When an eighth-note rest is placed within the triplet bracket, it becomes an eighth-note triplet rest. The missing syllable is a place marker.

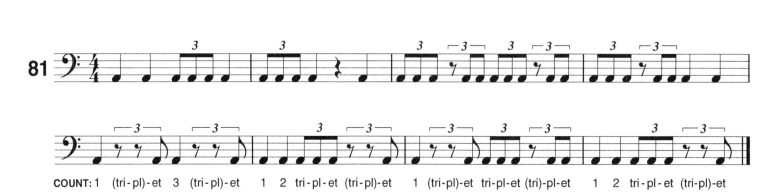

This bass line has a 12/8 feel. Notice how the drum part breaks up the beat with triplets on the hi-hat.

THE '50S

TRACK 44

12/8 TIME

Sometimes, triplet-based music is notated in **12/8 time**. In 12/8, there are twelve eighth notes in each measure. However, the dotted quarter note (♩.) gets the emphasis—so the feel is still essentially four beats per measure, with each beat divided into three eighth notes.

This movable box shape line takes advantage of the open D string to facilitate the position shift.

BUMPIN'

TRACK 45
SLOW/FAST

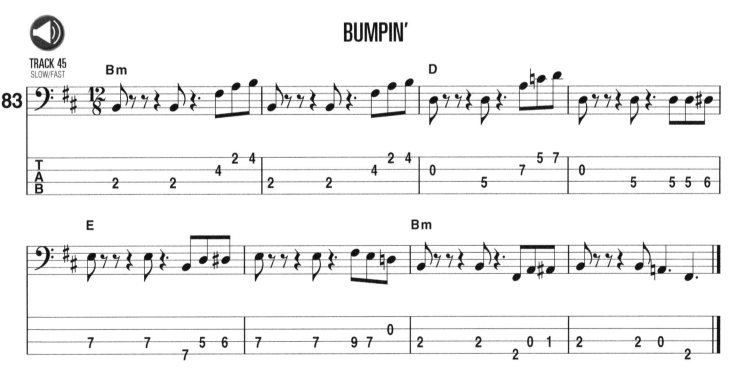

THE SHUFFLE RHYTHM

A popular rhythm based on eighth-note triplets is the **shuffle**. It is the foundation of most blues, as well as being used in many other styles. The shuffle uses the 1st and 3rd beats of an eighth-note triplet to create a familiar "stuttering" feel.

The shuffle can also be written and played with a longer, smoother feel. In this case, the first two beats of the eighth-note triplet are joined, adding up to a quarter note. Because triplets can be cumbersome to read, this feel is also sometimes notated simply as eighth notes, but with a shuffle indication ($\sqcap$ = $\sqcap$ ♪) at the start of the piece.

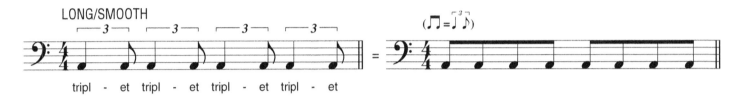

Here are some classic shuffle feels. This first one is of the "long/smooth" type.

OLD DAYS

TRACK 46

44

ONE- AND TWO-MEASURE REPEATS

The next example uses a notation shorthand called **one**- and **two-measure repeats**. They indicate to repeat either the previous one or two measures.

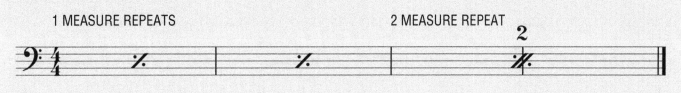

1 MEASURE REPEATS

2 MEASURE REPEAT

BAD BONE

TRACK 47
SLOW/FAST

85

Here is a box shape line that's been "shuffle-ized."

UPTOWN DOWN

TRACK 48

86

Here's shuffle-ized version of the classic blues line in A. This variation has the flatted 7th scale degree instead of the octave for the top note.

TRACK 49

CLASSIC FLAT 7

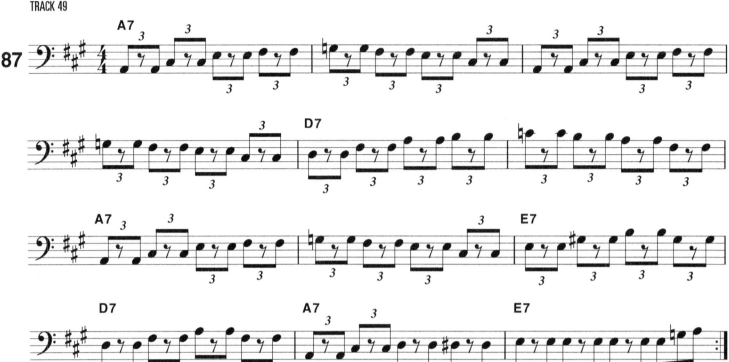

This tune has a gospel feel.

TRACK 50

ROLLIN'

GO ON

TRACK 51

HAL LEONARD

BASS METHOD

METHOD BOOKS

by Ed Friedland

BOOK 1

Book 1 teaches: tuning; playing position; musical symbols; notes within the first five frets; common bass lines, patterns and rhythms; rhythms through eighth notes; playing tips and techniques; more than 100 great songs, riffs and examples; and more! The audio includes 44 full-band tracks for demonstration or play-along.
00695067 Book Only.................................$7.99
00695068 Book/Online Audio...............$12.99

BOOK 2

Book 2 continues where Book 1 left off and teaches: the box shape; moveable boxes; notes in fifth position; major and minor scales; the classic blues line; the shuffle rhythm; tablature; and more!
00695069 Book Only.................................$7.99
00695070 Book/Online Audio...............$12.99

BOOK 3

With the third book, progressing students will learn more great songs, riffs and examples; sixteenth notes; playing off chord symbols; slap and pop techniques; hammer-ons and pull-offs; playing different styles and grooves; and more.
00695071 Book Only.................................$7.99
00695072 Book/Online Audio...............$12.99

COMPOSITE

This money-saving edition contains Books 1, 2 and 3.
00695073 Book Only...............................$17.99
00695074 Book/Online Audio...............$24.99

DVD

Play your favorite songs in no time with this DVD! Covers: tuning, notes in first through third position, rhythms through eighth notes, fingerstyle and pick playing, 4/4 and 3/4 time, and more! Includes 6 full songs and on-screen music notation. 68 minutes.
00695849 DVD.......................................$19.95

BASS FOR KIDS

by Chad Johnson

Bass for Kids is a fun, easy course that teaches children to play bass guitar faster than ever before. Popular songs such as "Crazy Train," "Every Breath You Take," "A Hard Day's Night" and "Wild Thing" keep kids motivated, and the clean, simple page layouts ensure their attention remains focused on one concept at a time.
00696449 Book/Online Audio $12.99

REFERENCE BOOKS

BASS SCALE FINDER

by Chad Johnson

Learn to use the entire fretboard with the *Bass Scale Finder*. This book contains over 1,300 scale diagrams for the most important 17 scale types.
00695781 6" x 9" Edition.......................$7.99
00695778 9" x 12" Edition.....................$7.99

BASS ARPEGGIO FINDER

by Chad Johnson

This extensive reference guide lays out over 1,300 arpeggio shapes. 28 different qualities are covered for each key, and each quality is presented in four different shapes.
00695817 6" x 9" Edition.......................$7.99
00695816 9" x 12" Edition.....................$7.99

MUSIC THEORY FOR BASSISTS

by Sean Malone

Acclaimed bassist and composer Sean Malone will explain the written language of music, using easy-to-understand terms and concepts, diagrams, and much more. The audio provides 96 tracks of examples, demonstrations, and play-alongs.
00695756 Book/Online Audio $17.99

STYLE BOOKS

BASS LICKS

by Ed Friedland

This comprehensive supplement to any bass method will help students learn over 200 great bass licks, lines and grooves in many rhythmic styles. *Bass Licks* illustrates how simple melodic patterns can become the springboard for group improvisation or the foundation of a song.
00696035 Book/Online Audio $14.99

BASS LINES

by Matt Scharfglass

500 expertly written bass lines, riffs and fills in a wide variety of musical genres are included in this comprehensive collection to help players expand their bass vocabulary. The examples cover many tempos, keys and feels, and include easy bass lines for beginners on up to advanced riffs for more experienced bassists.
00148194 Book/Online Audio $19.99

BLUES BASS

by Ed Friedland

Learn to play studying the songs of B.B. King, Stevie Ray Vaughan, Muddy Waters, Albert King, the Allman Brothers, T-Bone Walker, and many more. Learn riffs from blues classics including: Born Under a Bad Sign • Hideaway • Hoochie Coochie Man • Killing Floor • Pride and Joy • Sweet Home Chicago • The Thrill Is Gone • and more.
00695870 Book/Online Audio $14.99

COUNTRY BASS

by Glenn Letsch

21 songs, including: Act Naturally • Boot Scootin' Boogie • Crazy • Honky Tonk Man • Love You Out Loud • Luckenbach, Texas (Back to the Basics of Love) • No One Else on Earth • Ring of Fire • Southern Nights • Streets of Bakersfield • Whose Bed Have Your Boots Been Under? • and more.
00695928 Book/Online Audio $17.99

FRETLESS BASS

by Chris Kringel

18 songs, including: Bad Love • Continuum • Even Flow • Everytime You Go Away • Hocus Pocus • I Could Die for You • Jelly Roll • King of Pain • Kiss of Life • Lady in Red • Tears in Heaven • Very Early • What I Am • White Room • more.
00695850...$19.99

FUNK BASS

by Chris Kringel

This is your complete guide to learning the basics of grooving and soloing funk bass. Songs include: Can't Stop • I'll Take You There • Let's Groove • Stay • What Is Hip • and more.
00695792 Book/Online Audio...............$22.99

R&B BASS

by Glenn Letsch

This book/audio pack uses actual classic R&B, Motown, soul and funk songs to teach you how to groove in the style of James Jamerson, Bootsy Collins, Bob Babbitt, and many others. The 19 songs include: For Once in My Life • Knock on Wood • Mustang Sally • Respect • Soul Man • Stand by Me • and more.
00695823 Book/Online Audio $17.99

ROCK BASS

by Sean Malone

This book/audio pack uses songs from a myriad of rock genres to teach the key elements of rock bass. Includes: Another One Bites the Dust • Beast of Burden • Money • Roxanne • Smells like Teen Spirit • and more.
00695801 Book/Online Audio...............$21.99

SUPPLEMENTARY SONGBOOKS

These great songbooks correlate with Books 1-3 of the *Hal Leonard Bass Method*, giving students great songs to play while they're still learning! The audio tracks include great accompaniment and demo tracks.

EASY POP BASS LINES

20 great songs that students in Book 1 can master. Includes: Come as You Are • Crossfire • Great Balls of Fire • Imagine • Surfin' U.S.A. • Takin' Care of Business • Wild Thing • and more.
00695810 Book Only.............................$9.99
00695809 Book/Online Audio...............$15.99

MORE EASY POP BASS LINES

20 great songs for Level 2 students. Includes: Bad, Bad Leroy Brown • Crazy Train • I Heard It Through the Grapevine • My Generation • Pride and Joy • Ramblin' Man • Summer of '69 • and more.
00695819 Book Only...........................$12.99
00695818 Book/Online Audio...............$16.99

EVEN MORE EASY POP BASS LINES

20 great songs for Level 3 students, including: ABC • Another One Bites the Dust • Brick House • Come Together • Higher Ground • Iron Man • The Joker • Sweet Emotion • Under Pressure • more.
00695821 Book.....................................$9.99
00695820 Book/Online Audio...............$16.99

Visit Hal Leonard online at
www.halleonard.com

Prices, contents and availability subject to change without notice.
Some products may not be available outside of U.S.A.